This Book Belongs To

_____

On Applegate Farm, standing in the middle of the old wooden barn is a little red tractor called Toby.
The sunbeams from the early morning sunrise shone brightly through the gaps in the wooden walls of the old barn. Toby was the brightest colour in the barn, his red body and black wheels shone so brightly.

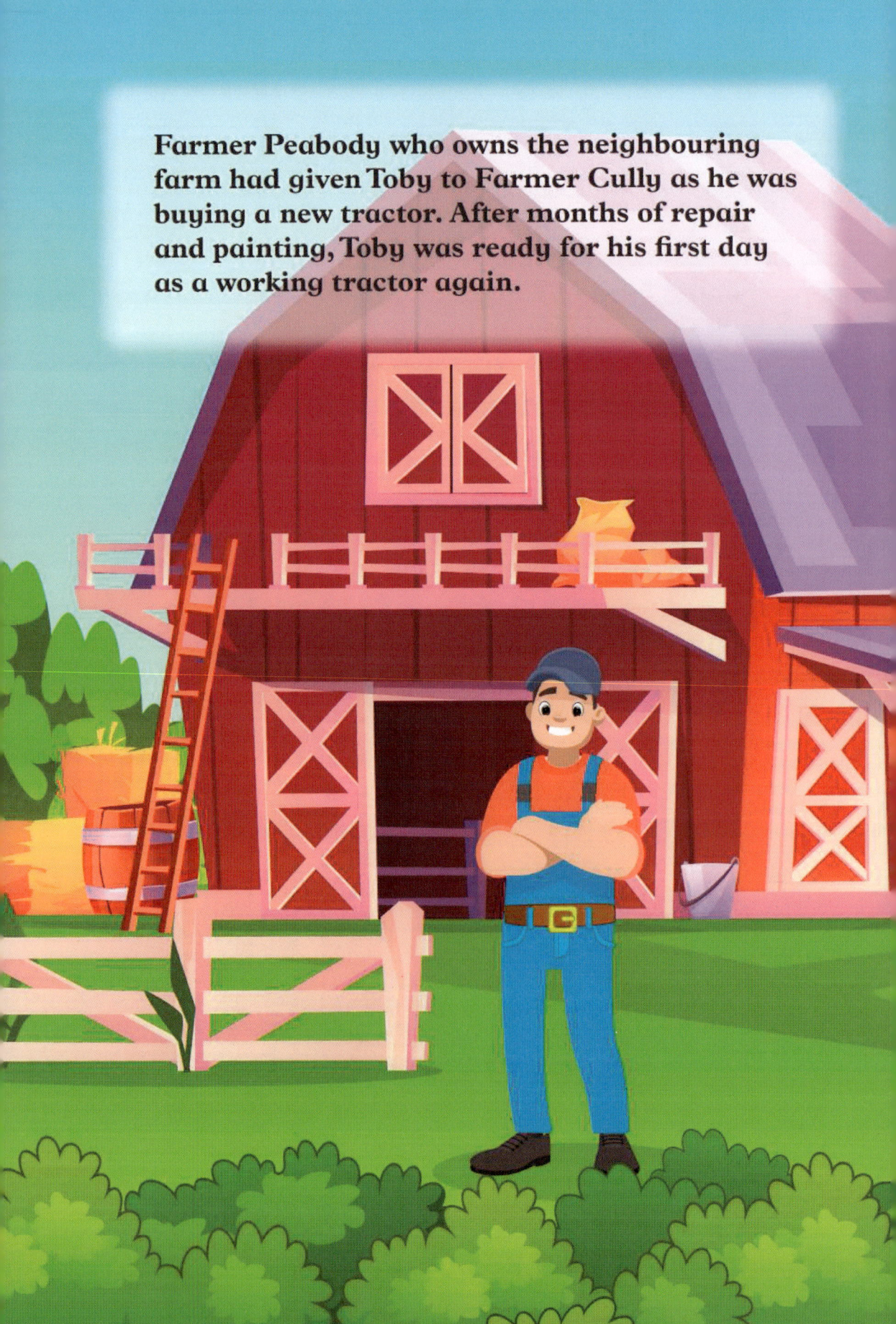

Farmer Peabody who owns the neighbouring farm had given Toby to Farmer Cully as he was buying a new tractor. After months of repair and painting, Toby was ready for his first day as a working tractor again.

The huge barn doors flew open and there stood Farmer Cully, who was just as excited as Toby. Come on Toby let us move you out into the yard.
He pressed the large starter button and Toby roared into action. This was going to be a very good day thought the little tractor.

As Toby moved forward he felt a tickle in his tummy which was where Farmer Cully had replaced the torn covering that was shelter for the driver in bad weather. The little tractor gave a wiggle and it seemed to stop. Nothing to worry about he thought to himself must be my new cover tickling me.

Toby stood gleaming with pride; he must surely be the most handsome tractor in the whole wide world he thought to himself. Two enormous black tyres at the back of him and two smaller ones at the front. Toby thought how clever Farmer Cully was to choose such a bright red for his body and a shiny silver exhaust was the finishing touch.

The little tractor didn't much fancy collecting rubbish all day, he wanted to plough the field instead.
After years of being left in a corner gathering rust by his previous owner, Toby wanted to show off a little with his shiny paint and new tyres.

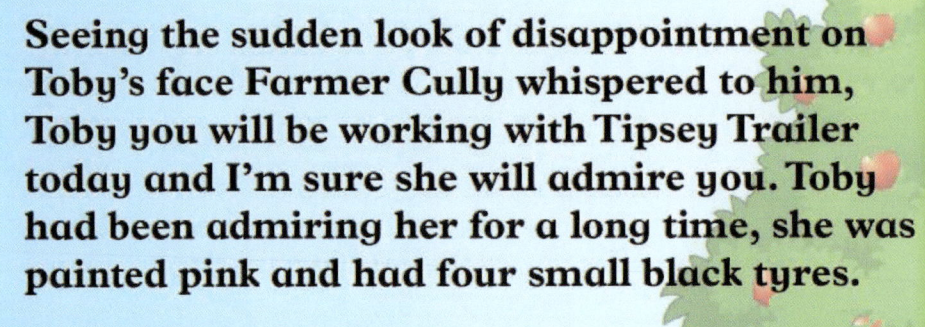

Seeing the sudden look of disappointment on Toby's face Farmer Cully whispered to him, Toby you will be working with Tipsey Trailer today and I'm sure she will admire you. Toby had been admiring her for a long time, she was painted pink and had four small black tyres.

There had been an accident in the barn one day when Derek the Digger reversed into Tipsey leaving her with one wobbly wheel at the back.
Although the wheel wobbled it was not loose so it was considered to be quite safe as it was. Derek had never really apologised for his mistake and often made jokes about the wobbly wheel when Farmer Cully wasn't there. Derek was not very nice at all. Derek was taller than the others and had a deep voice that seemed to make the old barn shudder.

Toby and Tipsey were locked together and ready for their day's work ahead. Toby was to pull the little trailer along behind him and she would carry the rubbish and twigs they collected along the way. The two had become good friends over the past four months.
I had the same treatments as you said Tipsey in her soft voice, my first day at work here after being painted and polished was so exciting too

Toby thought her voice was so pretty
and soft as fluffy clouds on a summer's day.
The little red tractor didn't mind collecting
rubbish now as he would be with Tipsey.
Derek was not needed for work today and the
others were happy to leave him behind.
He could stay in the barn today on his own.

Toby was looking forward to showing Tipsey how strong, bright and clever he was. Suddenly, there it was again, the tickling in his tummy. Toby wriggled a little to try and ease the tickle. Tipsey felt the wriggle but thought it was just her wobbly wheel. It stopped

Toby wasn't sure he was going to like the new covering if it was going to tickle. Farmer Cully was ready to start work now so he pressed the big start button and off the three of them went down the pathway and along the narrow lane to start work on the hedgerows that surrounded the fields.

Derek the Digger was finding it a little too quiet all alone in the barn.
Derek had been working all Winter on potholes around the farm and lanes nearby, on loan to Farmer Peabody. The farm was on a steep hill and the hedgerows along the edge of the field had gathered lots of rubbish and twigs during winter, making the field and lanes look untidy.

Along the way they were joined by Ned, a young lad who often helped Farmer Cully with odd jobs around the farm when he stayed with his nan during school holidays.
This was February half term and the two of them had arranged for Ned to help for a couple of days. He was a polite young man, 14 years old, tall and rather thin with lots of wild-looking red hair. Ned was a good worker. The four of them worked hard all morning and were soon going to be at the end of the hedgerow when it happened.

Tipsey was now quite full, there had been lots of rubbish for Ned to collect along the way.
The wobbly wheel seemed to wobble a lot more as the trailer was nearly full and very heavy. Suddenly, it seemed to appear from nowhere, a delivery lorry came speeding down the lane.
These lanes were not built for big lorries, they simply aren't wide enough said Farmer Cully angrily.

Toby moved as fast as he could, to pull Tipsey into the hedgerow to make room for the lorry to pass by.
Toby did not see the huge pothole there that Derek had missed. The lorry drove past them and was gone as quickly as it appeared.

Down into the huge pothole went one side of Tipsey her shiny black wobbly wheel was off and rolling down the lane, stopping in the hedgerow at the bottom of the lane with a thud.
Tipsey laid in the pothole half in and half out. The pink paint of her trailer was covered in mud and scratches ran down her side.
Tears were rolling down her pretty face. Toby was stopped in front of her almost too scared to look at the damage caused by the pothole.

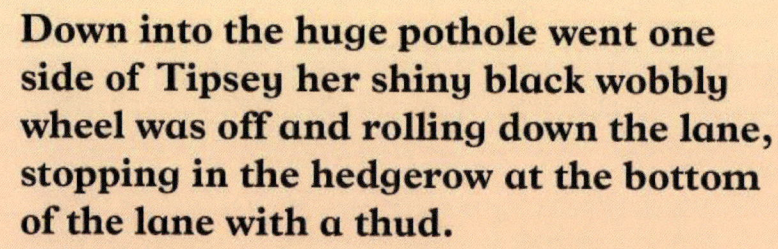

The rescue began, Farmer Cully gave Toby the order to pull as hard as he could, to lift Tipsey out of the pothole.
The little red tractor pulled and pulled with all his might. Toby's new tyres had a good grip to them, as he pulled and pulled over and over again. Toby was not leaving this job until Tipsey was free.

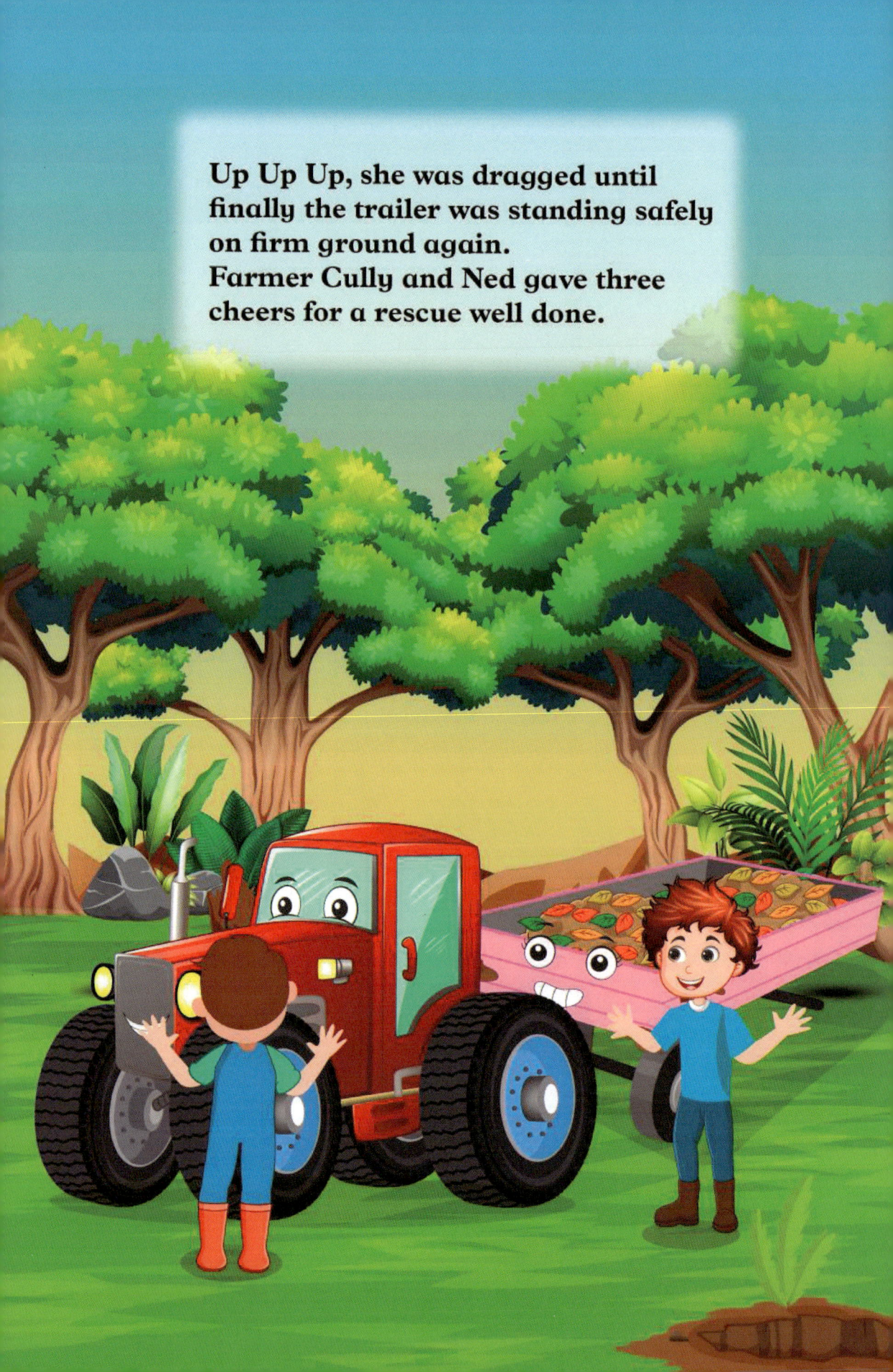

Up Up Up, she was dragged until finally the trailer was standing safely on firm ground again.
Farmer Cully and Ned gave three cheers for a rescue well done.

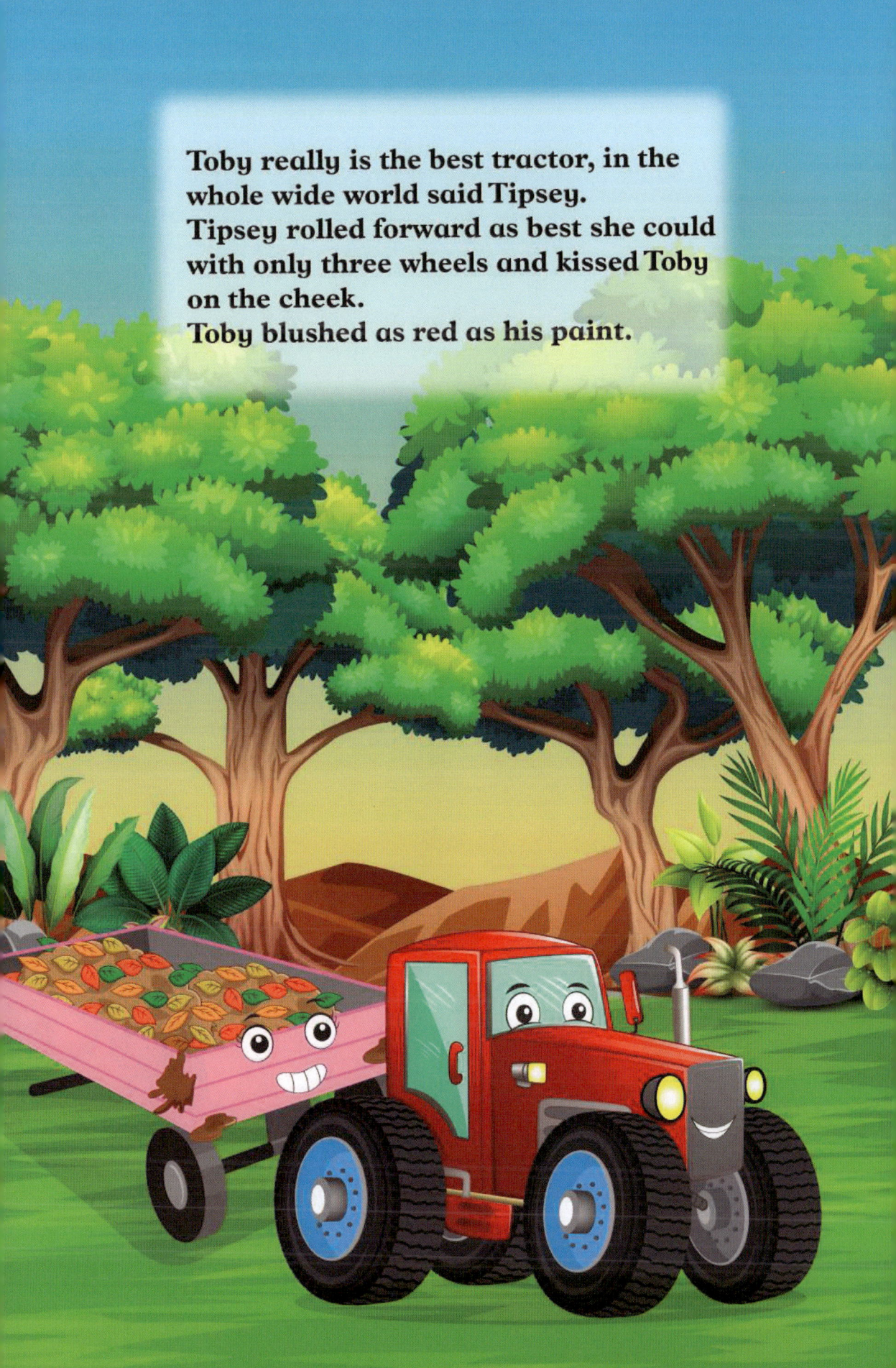

Toby really is the best tractor, in the whole wide world said Tipsey.
Tipsey rolled forward as best she could with only three wheels and kissed Toby on the cheek.
Toby blushed as red as his paint.

They drove very slowly down the lane back to the safety of the barn.
Farmer Cully reassured Tipsey that he would paint and repair her quickly.
On hearing the news Derek remembered showing off when he was working on the potholes. He was to blame. Not wanting to be in trouble with Farmer Cully he decided to be polite and say well done little tractor you were very brave and strong today.

Farmer Cully turned to Derek and said, you missed a pothole Derek. Tomorrow Derek you can clear all of the spilled rubbish and repair the pothole too. My apologies to you all said Derek shamefully and he sat quietly in the barn for the rest of the day without speaking or insulting anyone.

Ned was busy washing the mud off Tipsey when all of a sudden Toby let out a toot, toot of surprise. There it was, a little mouse peered through the window
of the covered cab where he had been hiding. That was Toby's tickle. Felix the field mouse had been living in Toby's cab for a while, protected from the cold winter. May I stay he asked I will try not to tickle too much in the future?

They all laughed, even Derek.

Printed in Great Britain
by Amazon